MAGICAL RITUALS FOR

MONEY

BY DONNA ROSE

ORIGINAL PUBLICATIONS
NEW YORK

MAGICAL RITUALS FOR MONEY

ISBN: 0-942272-78-1

Original Publications
P.O. Box 236
Old Bethpage, New York 11804-0236
1-888-OCCULT-1

TABLE OF CONTENTS

INTRODUCTION

This is a book of easy-to-do spells to obtain money or good luck. These traditional rituals and information have been used by practitioners for many generations. They have helped scores of people to improve their financial well being. Use them to help you obtain your goals.

Do not expect money and honors to just come to you of their own accord, just because you cast a spell. These spells and charms "aide", but must be employed in conjunction with your own positive actions to place yourself in a position where money and success are possible.

The secret to these workings is that they help you to send the thoughts and visions of success and money ahead of yourself, so that your following actions take you to the places and circumstances where these things are more readily available.

These formulas help your inner levels direct your feet to the places where money and your goals can be attained. Nothing more, nothing less! You have the ability to control your thoughts, which, in turn, enables you to fulfill your life dreams and help make a success of your life. The Spells are presented as a point of concentration which will assist you in sending out the most powerful thoughts.

Seals, talismans, stones, herbs and candleburning rituals all have magical powers within themselves; but, with your Positive Thinking and a useful objective, the power grows stronger.

The following rituals for obtaining money should he done on a Thursday at the hour of 7 P.M. Jupiter is the planet of wealth, and rules over Thursday. Seven (7) is the number for money and success. All rituals should be done in a series involving the 7 . . .7 days, 7 candles . . . 7 Incantations.

These rituals can be combined with the charms and used together-when so used, the power for obtaining money will be much stronger.

PRAYER FOR
PROTECTION

**I dwell in the bright, divine light,
All goodness is attracted to me for my highest good;
I am attuned with divine love and divine goodness . . .
I give thanks for the divine light.**

So Mote It Be.

THE LAW OF ABUNDANCE

This is also known by the name of the Law of Ten Fold. Any paper money that goes out will be affected. This also works with checks and money orders and credit cards (fold your receipt).

First, hold the bill in front of you. Use a $1 bill so you can see what I mean. Hold it so you can read the word "one dollar". This way it will come back to you. Faced in the other direction, you will notice it looks as though it is leaving. Now say to yourself:

Bless this money,
And as it goes out,
It comes back ten fold.

What it actually means in the first part is that you acknowledge where it comes from - God. The second line means you're manifesting it to come back now, not 20 years from now. The last part is "how" it will come back.

As you give someone the dollar, visualize ten dollars coming back to you at the same time, such as a ten dollar bill with wings coming over it towards you. It is said that this method will always work. Use it to increase your finance in business. Do this every single time you pay for anything.

CANDLEBURNING

The magical powers derived from candleburning come from the color of the candles, the incense, herbs and oils used, all combined in the Ritual. The ritual may be a complex one, or even a simple one with only one candle, but in essence, they still work on the same level.

Your state of mind is still the most important factor of your magical power. The importance of positive thinking while burning the candles insures the success of the Operation and the granting of your desire.

The one basic simple fact we can feel sure of is that the act of burning candles does indeed cause an altered state of awareness, producing changes in circumstances. Think of the millions of men and women who have been persuaded and seduced, or extracted promises and proposals, concluded business deals, patched up squabbles, and resolved differences of opinion in the glowing magic of a candlelight supper. Many a birthday wish has come true when all the candles were blown out!

DRESSING THE CANDLES

Candles should be anointed prior to use for vibrational energy. The oil needs to be harmonious thus it will be for the same purpose as your intent. It is extremely important that you cleanse the candle of any negative vibrations it might have absorbed from the many people that have handled it prior to your purchase. This is very simple. To banish negativity, first rub a little baby oil or virgin olive oil into the palms of your hands wipe one hand at a time from the base to the wick of the candle. You're done.

To bless or anoint (and you can use any size candle) for the purpose of your ritual use, starting from the middle of the candle, rub the oil upwards to the tip of the wick. Then starting once again from the middle, rub down to the bottom. Candles have polarity. Top is the "North Pole"; the bottom is the "South Pole".

You do not need to buy a candle at a religious store. It can be from the supermarket. The best are made from bees wax. The rest are paraffin or vegetable oil.

MONEY ATTRACTION

Light three candles placed next to each other three inches apart; the middle candle the color green, the two outside candles being white. Hold the object (a ring, talisman, coin, stone, etc.) that you want to energize over the middle flame by a rope, chain or string. Focus on what you want and feel the energy from your hands flow into the object as you repeat:

By the Power of God,
By ten times ten,
This (name the object, such as stone)
now a magnet shall be,
To attract money and wealth,
Be consecrated now unto me.

Partners now in growth we'll be,
And as my will, so mote it be!

FINANCIAL SUCCESS

To bring in financial success, burn a gold candle anointed with Success Oil. Read Psalm 150 from the Bible three times. Focus on the words.

RELEASE FROM MONEY DIFFICULTIES

Anoint a brown candle with Success Oil. Read Psalms 54 and 71 from the Bible. Use sincere prayer with this. Repeat each day until your result comes in.

SEVEN KNOB CANDLES FOR WISHING

The Seven Knob Candle is also called the "Wish" candle. For luck or money, use a green Seven Knob Candle.

For One Wish:

On parchment paper write your wish and place it beneath the candle. Each day burn one knob and focus on your wish.

More Than One Wish:

Write a separate wish on each of seven sheets of parchment paper. Tie or pin one wish to each knob on the candle. Burn one knob each day. As the knob with the wish is burned, the vibration goes out to attract your wish. Anoint the candle with an oil that matches your wish.

QUICK MONEY

Anoint a blue candle with Fast Luck Oil. Read Psalm 81 from the Bible each day until you receive your desires. This ritual can also be used for health to create blessings in the home.

BLACK CAT SPELL

Burn the Black Cat candle. Light it and while you focus on the flame, focus on good luck and money coming to you. Let the candle burn itself out.

INFLUENCE MONEY OPPORTUNITIES

Cover your altar with a white cloth. Place a religious symbol in the center of the altar and in front of it place some Good Luck incense. On the top right and left corners place a white candle anointed with All Purpose oil.

Anoint two green candles with Chinese Luck oil and place them on the bottom right and left corners Light the incense and candles and say this affirmation aloud:

I now attract what is mine by Divine Right.
I desire (fill in your desire).

Allow the candle to burn themselves out and be confident that money making opportunities will be presenting themselves to you soon.

ENSURE PROSPERITY

Follow these steps on a daily basis in your home or your place of business until your prosperity starts to come in. Burn an Orange Candle anointed with Prosperity Oil. Around the base of the candle sprinkle and burn Patchouli Incense. Sprinkle Sandalwood Powder around the premises. Wear the Prosperity Oil each day on your wrists and on your third eye (in the middle of your forehead).

ACHIEVE FINANCIAL SUCCESS

Utilize a white, green and pink candle. Anoint each with Almond Oil. Also add Almond Oil to Finance Drawing Incense. Focus on your intent. Do this for seven days.

TO GAIN MONEY

Cover your altar with a white cloth. Place a Bible in the center. On the left bottom corner place a white Crucifix Altar Candle dressed with High Altar Oil. Place a gold candle anointed with Money Drawing oil above it. Place two green candles dressed with Lady Luck oil on the right bottom corner. Read Psalm 41 from the Bible each day until you have accomplished your goal.

ALL GOOD FORTUNE

Burn a green candle anointed with Patchouli Oil. Read Psalms 73 to 83. When you are finished, say a prayer for the purpose you need to manifest. Do this as often as you wish until you have accomplished your goal. Remember always to thank the powers that be for their assistance.

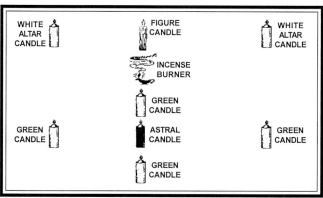

Materials:

1. Male or Female image candle; green in color
2. 2 White Altar candles (can be Stick Candle or Crucifix Candles)
3. Astral Candle *(your Astral color)*
4. 4 Green Stick Candles
5. Money Drawing Incense
6. Money Drawing Oil

Procedure:

1. Anoint the Green candles with the *Money Drawing* oil.
2. Light the *Money Drawing* incense.
3. Light the Altar Candles.
4. Light the Green candles.
5. Light the Astral Candle.
6. Chant the following Incantation three times:

Breath of Air, Drops of Water, Flame of fire, Dust of Earth
Carry the Money from There to Here, To come to me.
Green of Money, Green of Candles,
Money is needed, so come my way!
So Mote it Be!

Move each of the Green candles a little bit closer to
the Astral Candle each day.
Do the Ritual every day for at least 5 days.

TO OBTAIN A SPECIFIC FINANCIAL GAIN

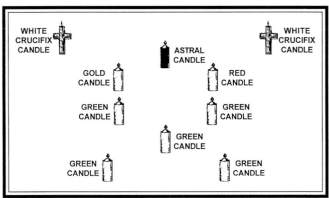

Materials:
1. Two White Crucifix Candles
2. One Astral Candle, your Astral Color
3. One Gold candle
4. Five Green Candles
5. One Red Candle
6. High Altar Oil
7. Zodiac Oil, your Sign
8. Glow of Attraction Oil
9. Money Drawing Oil
10. Commanding Oil

Procedure:
1. Anoint the Crucifix Candles with High Altar Oil
2. Light the Crucifix Candles
3. Anoint the Astral Candle with your Zodiac Oil
4. Light the Astral Candle.
5. Anoint the Gold candle with Glow of Attraction Oil.
6. Light the Gold candle.
7. Anoint the Green candles with the Money Drawing Oil.
8. Light the Green candles.
9. Anoint the Red candle with Commanding Oil.
10. Light the Red candle.
11. Allow the candles to burn for 20 minutes.
12. Meditate-think of, and visualize, the amount of money need.
13. Do the Ritual for three days in a row.

CANDLEBURNING TO ATTAIN SUCCESS

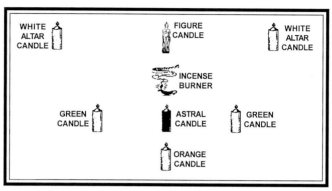

Materials:
1. Green Male or Female Image candle
2. Two White Altar Candles
3. Success Incense
4. Your Astral Candle
5. Three Orange candles
6. Success Oil

Procedure:
1. Anoint the Orange candles with Success Oil.
2. Anoint the Astral Candle with Success Oil.
3. Light the incense.
4. Light the Altar Candles.
5. Light the Orange candles.
6. Light the Astral Candle.
7. Chant:

Flame of my candles reach out,
And bring success to me.
Incense of success reach out,
And bring success to me.
Success is mine! Success is mine! Success is mine!
So Mote It Be!

8. Allow 15 minutes for the Ritual.
9. Think Positive for your desire.

CANDLEBURNING TO GAIN PROSPERITY

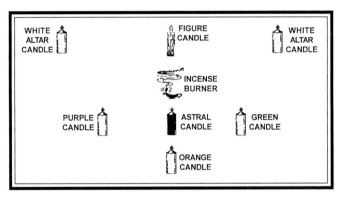

In the diagram:
- WHITE ALTAR CANDLE
- FIGURE CANDLE
- WHITE ALTAR CANDLE
- INCENSE BURNER
- PURPLE CANDLE
- ASTRAL CANDLE
- GREEN CANDLE
- ORANGE CANDLE

Materials:
1. Green Male or Female Image candle
2. Two White Altar Candles
3. Incense-Prosperity Drawing
4. Your Astral Candle
5. One Purple candle
6. One Green candle
7. One Orange candle
8. Prosperity Oil

Procedure:
1. Anoint all Candles with ProsperityOil.
2. Light Altar Candles.
3. Light the Prosperity Drawing incense.
4. Light Purple candle.
5. Light Orange candle.
6. Light Green candle.
7. Light Astral Candle.
8. Chant two times:

Attraction, Confidence, Money, Wealth, Progress,
Power, Prosperity;
The power within, the power of all.
These are mine,
Now, now, now!
So Mote It Be!

Allow 20 minutes for the Ritual.
Think Positive for your desire.

CANDLEBURNING - FINANCIAL GAIN

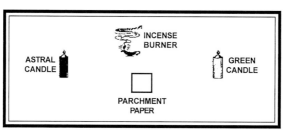

Materials:
1. Financial Luck Incense
2. Financial Luck Oil
3. Your Astral Candle
4. Green Candle
5. Parchment Paper
6. Black Ink

Procedure:
1. Anoint each Candle with Financial Luck Oil.
2. Write the amount of money you wish to receive on parchment paper.
3. Light the Financial Luck Incense.
4. Light Astral Candle.
5. Light Green candle.
6. After you light the candle, think of money in your hands; feel the money in your hands. Picture yourself spending the money.

Allow 20 minutes for the Ritual.
Think Positive for your desire.

WHAT ARE CHARM BAGS?

According to occult tradition they are a collection of natural odds and ends that have a mystical correspondence associated with the idea for which they are gathered.

Herbs, roots, stones, feathers, powders, bones, etc., etc. are gathered at the proper time and put together in a bag with the right intention held in mind to give it the natural magnetic charge for its purpose.

The Charm Bag acts as a solid condenser to help solidify the makes, thoughts and wishes to aid the psychic energy *which helps cause* changes according to will.

Follow the formulas and make the charms for yourself, your friends or clients.

Charge them by following the small Ceremony of Consecration You will then have a traditional and an authentic Witches Charm Bag.

CEREMONY OF CONSECRATION

At Midnight on the Day proscribed to make the charm bag, lay all of your ingredients on your altar and say:

CHARMS AND ENCHANTMENTS,
HERBS AND ROOTS,
STUFFED IN THIS BAG,
INTO WORKERS OF WONDER MY WILL TRANSMUTES.

Light a white candle and some Meditation incense. Place a chalice or bowl of pure water and a small dish of earth or salt next to the charm bag. Sprinkle the bag with a few drops of the water and a few grains of the earth or salt as you say:

BLESSED AND WASHED OF ALL THY PAST,
ONLY MY WILL UPON THEE WILL LAST.

Pass the bag through the fire three times. Then hold it in the rising incense smoke and say:

CHARM BAG I BID THEE TO WORK MY WILL,
TO KEEP THY INTENTION AS MY MAGIC'S MILL.
DO AS THOU ART RIGHTLY BID
WITH WITCHES CHARMS WITHIN THEE SAFELY HID.

Concentrate on your desire, or reason for the charm bag. Visualize it and breath that idea over the entire bag three times.

The bag may then be considered consecrated to its purpose. Let the candle and incense burn out.

LOW JOHN BAG

Materials:

1. 1 Red flannel bag
2. A Low John Conqueror root (ground)
3. A Blank Check (you can create your own)
4. Nutmeg Oil
5. Cinnamon Oil
6. Sandalwood Oil

Procedure:

1. Use Ceremony of Consecration for each oil , the Check and the Bag.

2. Make the check out to you, write the amount of money on the check that you need to pay your bill.

3. Anoint the check with each oil.

4. Place the check in the green bag along with ground Low John Root. Carry your bag with you in pocket or purse wherever you go.

ANOTHER LOW JOHN BAG

On a Thursday, when the moon is waxing, place the following items in a Green Bag:

1 Low John Root
1 Small Green Stone
Green Money Drawing Powder
1 teaspoon Yellow Mustard Seed

Tie the bag shut. Anoint the bag each Thursday with Money Drawing Oil.

MONEY DRAWING

On a Thursday, when the moon is waxing, place the following items in a Green Bag:

Fenugreek
Orris Root
Chamomile
Schemhamphoras Seal #1

1. Anoint the bag with Money Drawing Oil.

2. Anoint a green seven-day candle with Money Drawing oil, burn one knob each day.

3. While the candle burns anoint the bag with the same oil, contemplate on your desire as you do so.

FAST MONEY

Place the following items in a Red Pouch:

2 Lodestones
Horse Chestnut
1 Fixed Nutmeg
Fern
Woodruff

Anoint the pouch and its contents with Success Oil and Almond Oil. Wrap money around the bag and carry it.

LUCKY MONEY LAVENDER SPELL

Sprinkle seven types of money with Lavender Oil and place into a green conjure bag (one penny, one nickel, one dime, one quarter, one half dollar, one dollar bill, one five dollar bill).

Anoint your bag with Lavender Oil each day and take everywhere you go. It is said that your money should increase soon.

TO FIND MONEY

On a Thursday during a time when the Moon is waxing, in a Green Mojo Bag, place some Gold Magnetic Sand and the herb Smartweed. Write your name and birthdate on the back of the Seal of Treasure with a Quill pen and Dove's Blood Ink. Now write a short description of your prayer request or desire. Now do the same on the back of the Seal of Good Fortune. Anoint each seal with Jupiter Oil by placing a drop of each oil on each of the four corners. Place the seals in the bag and tie it shut. Anoint the mojo bag with Jupiter Oil. Carry it next to your wallet.

SEAL OF TREASURE

SEAL OF GOOD FORTUNE

MONEY BAG SPELL

Materials:

1. Several Silver or Gold colored coins
2. A Green Bag
3. Sandalwood Oil
4. Cinnamon Oil
5. Dragon's Blood Incense

Procedure:

1. Use Ceremony of Consecration to charge all objects.

2. Light the incense

3. Place the coins in the bag, anoint the bag and the coins with all three oils

4. Breath the incense in, drawing into your lungs as much of the incense as you can hold. Then take the bag and exhale into the bag onto the coins, and simply say:

Multiply!

5. Do this seven times, then close the bag.

6. Anoint the outside of the bag with each oil and place in a secret place in your home.

7. Keep your bag charged by anointing it periodically with the oils.

MONEY HOUSE BLESSING SPELL

Take four mojo bags the color of grass green.
In each bag place:

A one dollar bill
2 quarters
2 dimes
2 nickels
10 pennies

Place in the four mojo bags with the money:

1 Orris root
1 Buckeye
1 Pecan nut

Tie each bag with white thread three times.
While you tie the bag, focus on it and say:

Money to money,
Power to power,
Let the wealth that is mine,
Through Divine Right be showered,
Upon my home,
Upon my work,
Through rain and thunder,
From air to earth.

Take the bags and place each one into one of the four corners of your home. They can be placed somewhere that is not visual but in the open air, such as under a couch or in a potted plant.

Leave them there and visualize your home filled with money.

SIMPLE MAGICAL RECIPES
Oils, Incense, Body Lotions, Baths and Floorwash

BIG MONEY OIL
1 oz. Base Oil *(Jojoba, Sesame, Safflower or Almond Cooking Oil)*
9 drops Carnation Oil
9 drops Vanilla Oil
6 drops Lilac Oil
6 drops Sassafras Oil

FAST MONEY OIL
1 oz. Base Oil *(Jojoba, Sesame, Safflower or Almond Cooking Oil)*
15 drops Nutmeg Oil
9 drops Hyssop Oil
9 drops Honeysuckle Oil
9 drops Cinnamon Oil

LUCKY LOTTO OIL
1 oz. Base Oil *(Jojoba, Sesame, Safflower or Almond Cooking Oil)*
14 drops Allspice Oil
14 drops Sage Oil
14 drops Clover Oil
14 drops Cedarwood Oil

MONEY DRAWING OIL
1 oz. Base Oil *(Jojoba, Sesame, Safflower or Almond Cooking Oil)*
21 drops Sandalwood Oil
21 drops Jasmine Oil
14 drops Lime Oil
7 drops Bergamot Oil
7 drops Sweet Pea Oil
7 drops Peppermint Oil

THE GENERAL FORMULA FOR
MAKING SCENTED BODY LOTIONS

Body Lotions are a great way to anoint yourself with magical properties. Body Lotions can be applied daily after taking a ritual bath to ensure the maximum benefit of your desires.

1. *Place 1 cup of unscented body lotion or cream in a bowl.*
2. *Add all of the oils in the bowl.*
3. *Mix well and place the lotion in a sealed jar until ready to use.*

MONEY DRAWING
21 drops Coconut Oil
14 drops Peppermint Oil
7 drops Anise Oil

SUCCESS
21 drops Coconut Oil
14 drops Heather Oil
14 drops Nutmeg Oil

PROSPERITY
21 drops Violet Oil
14 drops Rose Oil
7 drops Cinnamon Oil
7 drops Pine Oil

BETTER BUSINESS
21 drops Heather Oil
14 drops Hyssop Oil
7drops Violet Oil
7 drops Coconut Oil

FAST MONEY
14 drops Cinnamon Oil
21 Hyssop Oil
7 drops Nutmeg Oil
7 drops Honeysuckle Oil

FAST LUCK
21 drops Patchouly Oil
7 drops Pine Oil
14 drops Vertivert Oil
7 drops Cinnamon Oil

LUCKY LOTTO
14 drops Sage Oil
14 drops Allspice Oil
14 drops Clover Oil
7 drops Civet Oil

THE GENERAL FORMULA FOR
MAKING POWDERED INCENSE

Incense is used by practioners of magic to enhance spells and communication with the spirits and gods. The following incenses are all made from natural ingredients. By burning natural ingredients, you are releasing the magical qualities of the herbs into the universe thus increasing the success rate of a magical spell or ritual. Because some of the following incenses are quite strong in fragrance, they should be burned in a well ventilated area.

1. *Mix all of the ingredients together.*
2. *Place the mixture into a glass storage jar until ready to use.*
3. *Burn 1 teaspoon at a time on a hot charcoal block.*

FAST LUCK / MONEY DRAWING INCENSE
3 oz. Cinnamon powder
1 oz. Cedarwood powder
1oz. Five Finger Grass
1 oz. High John the Conqueror Root powder

LUCKY LOTTO INCENSE
3 oz. Rue Herb
1 oz. Nutmeg pwdr.
2 oz. Cinnamon pwdr.
1 oz. Cedarwood pwdr.
2 oz. High John the Conqueror Root pwdr.
21drops Bergamot Oil
21drops Clover Oil
21 drops Heather Oil

BETTER BUSINESS INCENSE
3 oz. Cinnamon powder
1 oz. Allspice powder
1 oz. Cedarwood powder
1oz. Sandalwood powder
7 drops Money Drawing Oil
7drops Violet Oil
7 drops Vanilla Oil

THE GENERAL FORMULA FOR MAKING FLOOR WASHES

Spiritualists believe that by washing an area with a specially prepared herbal mixture they are bringing out the magical properties of the herbs which make up the floor wash. Floor washes can be used for such things as to attract love, luck, money and for protection. Many spiritualists believe that floor washes will enhance a magical spell and bring about better results.

1. *Boil all of the ingredients for 20 minutes in 1 quart of water.*
2. *Allow the liquid mixture to cool.*
3. *Add 1 cup of ammonia to the liquid mixture.*
4. *Pour the liquid mixture into a storage bottle until ready to use.*
5. *Allow the mixture to remain in bottle for 7 days before using.*

PROSPERITY
1 oz. Uva Ursa
1 oz. Bay Leaves
1 oz. Cinnamon Sticks
2 oz. Florida Water

FAST LUCK
1 oz. Cloves
1 oz. Rosemary
1 oz. Chamomile
1 oz. Marigold Flowers
2 oz. White Vinegar

BETTER BUSINESS
1 oz. Cinnamon powder
1 oz. Brown Sugar
1 oz. Allspice powder
1 oz. Rose Petals
2 oz. Kolonia 1800

FAST MONEY
1 oz. Pine Needles
1 oz. Patchouly Root
1 oz. Peppermint leaves
1 oz. Lavender
1 oz. Basil
2 oz. Kolonia 1800

THE GENERAL FORMULA FOR
MAKING BATH CRYSTALS

1. *Place 3 1/2 cups Kosher Rock Salt in a mixing bowl.*
2. *Add 2 cups Baking Soda to the mixing bowl.*
3. *Add 1/2 cup Sea Salt to the mixing bowl.*
4. *Add the ingredients listed in the recipe to the mixing bowl.*
5. *If desired, you may color the crystals with food coloring.*
6. *Mix and store in a storage jar until ready to use. Add 4-6 tablespoons to your bath. Immerse yourself completely, then soak for 10-20 minutes concentrationg on your desire.*

MONEY DRAWING SALT
1/2 oz. Cinnamon oil
1/2 oz. Nutmeg oil
1/2 oz. Peppermint oil

PROSPERITY BATH SALT
1/2 oz. Cinnamon oil
1/2 oz. Bayberry oil
1/2 oz. Nutmeg oil
1/2 oz. Sandalwood oil

BETTER BUSINESS
1/2 oz. Bayberry oil
1/2 oz. Bergamot oil
1/2 oz. Honeysuckle oil
1/2 oz. Mint oil

GET A JOB
1/2oz. Allspice oil
1/2 oz. Cinnamon oil
1/2 oz. Geranium oil

GAMBLING SALT
1/2 oz. Cinnamon oil
1/2 oz. Five Finger Grass oil
1/2 oz. Wintergreen oil

GIVE ME YOUR MONEY
1/2 oz. Angelica oil
1/2 oz. Ginseng oil
1/2 oz. Patchouli oil
1/2 oz. Cedarwood oil

SUCCESS
1/2 oz. Coconut oil
1/2 oz. Nutmeg oil
1/2 oz. Heather oil
1/2 oz. Mint oil

LUCKY LOTTERY
1/2oz. Allspice oil
1/2 oz. Sage oil
1/2 oz. Clover oil
1/2 oz. Cedarwood oil

SEALS

A Seal is a magical incantation inscribed on a sheet of parchment paper, which stands for or suggests a specific objective, reason or purpose.

The Seal is used as a magical tool for you. You must make a copy of the Seal yourself in order for the power of the symbol to bring you what it represents. One drawn or printed by someone else will not work as well.

As in all magical work, your state of mind is the most important mystical power of all, and your Positive Thinking is what will principally function to bring you the successful fulfillment of your desire.

All of the Seals should be anointed with the appropriate Oil as described in the accompanying text.

A knowledge of some of the ancient alphabets-notably Hebrew and Greek-will enable you to design your own Seals. In most magical Work, the personal touch is the way to make the most powerful tool.

If you plan on making several Seals, it's a good idea to buy a pen especially for the purpose, and reserve it for your magic work. Don't use it for everyday writing. Many folks believe a dip-style pen is best.

MONEY ATTRACTION RUNE

Focus on your intent as you do the following:

Trace the runes
Dove's Blood ink.

Trace the other symbols within the circle in green. Also trace the circle itself in green.

Now consecrate this talisman according to your chosen formula.

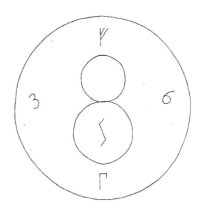

PROSPERITY DRAWING SIGIL RUNE

Focus on your intent.

Trace the symbol within the circle in Dove's Blood ink.

Hold it in your hand and focus the intent as long as you are able to.

Now use the method you would feel best with to consecrate it.

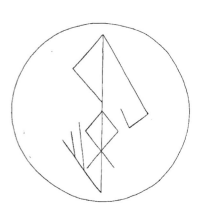

RUNIC TALISMAN FOR HAPPINESS, ABUNDANCE, PROSPERITY MAGNET

Focus on your intent.

Trace the pyramid within the circle in black.

Trace all other symbols in bright red.

Consecrate the talisman with the method of your choice.

THE ISLAMIC WEALTH TALISMAN

To be carried or worn for wealth and prosperity and good fortune. It is said, "Prosperous are the believers". It consists of a sickle-shaped moon with a five pointed star drawn within the open part of the sickle on the right side.

FOR GAINING BUSINESS SUCCESS

Materials:
1. Red Ink
2. Parchment Paper
3. Success Oil

Procedure:
1. Copy this Seal with Red ink onto a piece of Parchment Paper.
2. Anoint the Seal with Success Oil and put the completed Seal into your register or cash box.

Do not remove it from the register or cash box at any time.

FOR GAMBLING

Relates to all Gambling and Chance-Taking for Success

Materials:
1. Red Ink
2. Parchment Paper
3. Money Drawing Oil
4. Red Conjure Bag

Procedure:
1. Copy the Seal in Red Ink on Parchment Paper.
2. Anoint it with Money Drawing Oil.
3. Place it in a Red Conjure Bag
4. Hold the Conjure Bag in your hand for two hours and think of money.
5. Place the Conjure Bag somewhere on your body where it will be in contact with your skin (on a cord, around your neck, under your shirt or blouse is also good).

TO RECEIVE MONEY

Materials:
1. Dove's Blood Ink
2. Green Conjure Bag
3. Fast Luck Oil
4. Large Green Candle

Procedure:
1. Copy this Seal with Dove's Blood Ink on Parchment Paper.
2. Put the Seal in a Green Conjure Bag.
3. Anoint the bag with Fast Luck Oil.
4. Light a large Green candle, and place the bag in front of it. Allow the candle to burn out completely.
5. After the candle has gone out, put the bag in your pocket, and carry it with you at all times. After you do this, you will find that you always have some money on you.

TO OBTAIN MONEY IN A COURT CASE

Materials:
1. Parchment Paper
2. Success Oil
3. Large Brown Candle
4. Court Oil
5. Red Conjure Bag

Procedure:
1. Copy the Seal on Parchment Paper.
2. Anoint the Seal with Success Oil.
3. Place the Seal under a large Brown candle.
4. Anoint the candle with Court Oil.
5. Burn the candle.
6. Place the Seal in a Red Conjure Bag, and carry it with you when you go to court.

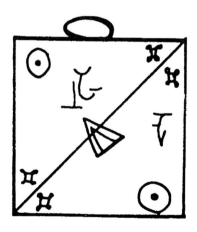

TO GET MONEY FROM OTHERS

Materials:
1. Parchment Paper
2. Dove's Blood Ink
3. Money Drawing Oil
4. Large Orange Energy Candle
5. Control Oil

Procedure:
1. Copy the Seal with Dove's Blood Ink on Parchment Paper.
2. Anoint the Seal with Money Drawing Oil.
3. Place it under a large Orange Energy Candle.
4. Anoint the candle with Control Oil.
5. Burn the candle.
6. Think of the person who is to give you the money. Fold up the Seal and carry it in your wallet.

FOR FAST LUCK

Materials:
1. Black Ink
2. Parchment Paper
3. Fast Luck Oil
4. One Dollar Bill

Procedure:
1. Copy this Seal, using Black ink on Parchment Paper.
2. Anoint the Seal with Fast Luck Oil.
3. Wrap the Seal around a dollar bill and place it in your wallet before you go out.

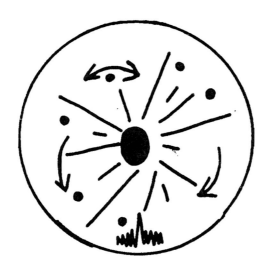

HERBAL CHARMS

1. **Black Snake Root** - Will lead money your way. Carry with you in a Green Conjure Bag.

2. **Buckeye** - Will attract wealth to you. Wrap it in a dollar bill and place in a Green Conjure Bag.

3. **Chamomile** - Before playing any games of chance, wash your hands in a cup of water with some Chamomile in it.

4. **Clover** - For financial matters. Place some in your bath water and bathe before attending to any financial matters.

5. **Coltsfoot** - For wealth and prosperity. Place some leaves in Green Conjure Bag and hang over your doorway.

6. **Dragon's Blood Reed** - To lure untold riches to you. Place a piece in a Green Conjure Bag and carry with you constantly.

7. **Fenugreek** - Brings money into your home. Leave a few seeds in an open jar in your house.

8. **High John The Conqueror** - Brings luck to gamblers. Boil the root in water, then wash your hands in the water before you gamble.

10. Lovage - Draws customers into your store. Sprinkle by your door and let prospective customers walk over it.

11. Low John The Conqueror - Causes money to increase. Place the root in a Green Conjure Bag and carry with your change.

12. Nutmeg - Brings fortune to you. On a piece of Parchment Paper, write in Dove's Blood Ink the amount of money you wish to come your way. Wrap the Parchment around a whole Nutmeg and carry with your change.

13. Ruler's Root - Brings luck your way. Place some in the four corners of each room in your house.

14. Scullcap - Inspires others to give you money. Place some Scullcap in a small saucer and moisten with Money Drawing Oil.

15. Smartweed - To find money. Place some Smartweed in a Green Conjure Bag along with a Lodestone and Gold Magnetic Sand.

16. Tonka Beans - To draw money your way. Place a pair of Tonka Beans in a Green Conjure Bag and carry with you.

MORE MISCELLANEOUS CHARMS

1. Carry this Charm with you when looking for a job. Take some powdered or dried **Red Clover** and place in a **Red Conjure Bag**. Anoint the bag with **Fast Luck Oil**.

2. Wear this Charm around your neck when you go looking for a job. Tie a piece of **white string** around a piece of **Devil's Shoestring Root** and wear around your neck.

3. Another job-finding Charm can be made by putting some **Chamomile Flowers** in a **Red Conjure Bag**, and wearing around your neck.

4. If you'd rather not wear a Charm, you can take the **Chamomile Flowers**, boil them in rain water, and, after the water has cooled, wash your hands with it. Then go out to apply for the job you want.

5. To draw money, take a **Green candle** and anoint it with **Money Drawing Oil.** Place a **Jezebel Root** under or by the candle, in such a way that the wax will drip on it when the candle burns. Burn the candle completely, then place the root and the wax sticking to it into a **Green Conjure Bag**, and carry it with you.

6. Wrap a dollar bill around a piece of **High John The Conqueror Root**, tie a **white string** around them to hold them together. Put in a **Green Conjure Bag**.

7. Burn a **Green 7 Knob Candle** which has been anointed with Money Drawing Oil.

8. Boil a **High John the Conqueror Root** in some water. Then wash your hands with the water before handling any money.

SPELL WHEN BUSINESS IS POOR

Before opening the front door at your shop, sprinkle some **Jinx Removing Salts**, then sweep away from your door.

Money Drawing Powder should be sprinkled by your front door (on the inside of your shop) so people will walk over it.

A trail of **Silver Magnetic Sand** should be sprinkled from the front door to your cash register.   *Think Positive for your desire.*

SPELL TO OBTAIN MONEY

Place a **Green Lodestone** in a **Red Conjure Bag** and put a piece of **Patchouli Herb** over it. Anoint the Bag with **Money Drawong Oil**, and then tie it up. Put the bag in a dark place for 7 days where no one will touch it.

At the end of the seventh day, take it out and carry it with you, either in your pocket, or your clothing.   *Money will come to you.*

SPELL FOR GAMBLING

Set a large **Green candle** on a table, place a **Green Lodestone** in front of it. Anoint the candle with **Gambling Oil.** Light the candle and allow it to burn for at least one hour.

Before going out to gamble, place the **Lodestone** in your pocket with your money. It will attract more money to come and join the money in your pocket.

WORKING WITH THE PSALMS

The following pages contain a variety of uses to which the psalms have been applied. By saying the particular psalm over and over with an intent, a specific purpose may be achieved.

When utilizing the psalms to achieve your goals it is vital that your purpose is stated specifically both before and after reading the psalm aloud.

PSALM #4

WIN A CONTEST OR LOTTERY - On a Friday, light a Green candle and pray this psalm along with the following affirmation out loud, eight times each, as the candle burns.

"O Lady Luck come to me now, and bring me what I need.
I've got the Sun, I want the Rain, I've planted all my seed.
So bring me a WIN and let me cash in, the tickets I now hold.
For I promise you I'll do my share,
to help others still out in the cold!"

GAIN GOOD LUCK - Write your name on a piece of parchment paper, wrap it in a dollar bill, carry it in your billfold and you will have good luck. Say the psalm each morning and anoint the bill to charge it up again.

PSALM #28

GAIN FINANCIAL SUCCESS - Burn a Green candle each night for five nights before going into a new venture. This will insure lasting success.

PSALM #35

GET FINANCIAL ASSISTANCE - Burn a Green candle anointed with Financial Oil, and your money request will be granted. Anoint a $10 bill and carry it in your wallet at all times. More money will flow to you.

PSALM 45

GET MONEY FROM YOUR MATE - Write the 2nd and 3rd verses on parchment paper and place it under his or her pillow. Do this for 3 nights in a row and you will receive some money.

PSALM #67

FOR FINANCIAL BLESSINGS - Get a handkerchief and a small towel. Put them both in a bowl and pour three bottles of Glory Water on them. As you rinse the articles in the Glory Water, recite the psalm out loud 3 times. Hang the handkerchief and the bath towel out to dry. Use the handkerchief and towel just as you normally would, but be sure that no one else uses these articles.

PSALM #72

FIND MONEY - Stand by an open window and read the psalm. Small amounts of money will flow your way.

PSALM #73

WIN AT THE HORSES - Write verses 5 and 6 on a dollar bill. Rub the bill on the program and you will pick the lucky numbers.

WIN A LOTTERY - Burn a Green candle on a piece of Green cloth, write the psalm on Parchment paper and burn it in the flame. Save the ashes and rub them on your tickets when you buy them. Allow no one else to touch the tickets, place them somewhere safe.

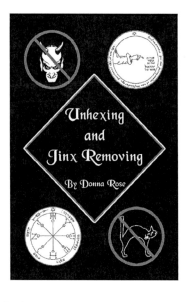

UNHEXING AND
JINX REMOVING

BY DONNA ROSE

Everywhere we turn these days it seems as if there are forces working against us. You don't need to spend your time thinking, worrying about or stressing over the evils that are constantly prowling. Cast out all forces of negativity, evil thoughts, evil intentions, evil spirits and so on. Break up conspiracies, dispel rumors, blanket your enemies with suffering and confusion. Believe it or not there are ways to protect yourself in this modern world. The easy to perform rituals and spells provided in this book will allow you to escape the dangers hounding you.

ISBN 0-942272-84-6 5½"x 8½" $6.95

ITEM #224
$6.95

Revised and Expanded

Success and Power Through Psalms

By Donna Rose

For thousands of years, men and women have found in the Psalms the perfect prayer book, possessing wisdom applicable to every human situation. Wise men and women of deep mystical insight have also learned to decipher the magical formulas David and the other Psalmists hid behind the written words. These formulas help the seeker solve everyday problems, achieve higher states of consciousness, gain material and spiritual wealth, as well as help defend himself or herself against psychic attacks and all manner of dangers.

The Revised and Expanded edition of Donna Rose's classic offers over 300 simple to perform magical rituals to help you manifest all of your desires using the magical powers of the psalms.

ISBN 0-942272-79-X 5½"x 8½ $6.95